Gallery Books
Editor Peter Fallon

SELECTED POEMS

Seán Lysaght

SELECTED POEMS

Gallery Books

Selected Poems
is first published
simultaneously in paperback
and in a clothbound edition
on 7 October 2010.

The Gallery Press
Loughcrew
Oldcastle
County Meath
Ireland

www.gallerypress.com

ISBN 978 1 85235 501 2 *paperback*
    978 1 85235 502 9 *clothbound*

A CIP catalogue record for this book
is available from the British Library.

(*Noah's Irish Ark* was published
by The Dedalus Press in 1989.)

Contents

for Daniel

Before Anthropology

Before the first words in Ireland
there were sparse, post-glacial trees,
and northern birds.

Before the hunched primates
of the Bann and their caravan
of history

there were sub-arctic vistas:
herring grounds,
and tundra hills unnamed.

I take palaeo-paths
after Praeger and de Buitléar
into rugged interiors,

or down to the rim of the sea,
to the lost boreal continents
before me and my story

where there's no freezing bivouac,
no manned anorak
between me and the loon.

Our archaeology begins
in the first settlings
of birch pollen;

the bone we know
is a bear dying in a cave
long ago.

Before I get to the museum
new broadleaves come hither
in milder weather.

Coracles reach a northern shore
loaded with term and totem,
and hatch my kind.

Much blood has dried
in the long chronicle
of passion, hate and vanity.

It's all there in the archives
I have served —
and will serve again;

because there's more to do
and more to say, says a friend
who's great of heart.

And in all I do
and say there's the scene
the heart prefers,

of that first loneliness
of trees
and northern birds.

The Haggard

1

There was something I had
to find out, so I ran
down the dim
orifice of memory

to stand, where my uncle had stood,
pike in hand, before
the first box-camera
in the parish.

I was barefoot
and brazen as the kin
untying the gate
into the haggard.

The hay in the shed smoked
when I brushed it.
Turnips and mangels lay
in the pits, sure

of being redeemed. A shot
of finches fled my wonder
and withdrew into
a loaded apple tree.

I came back to the store
of the heart; to its seed,
massed like the seed
at the core of the oat-stack;

to the hard
adequacies my blood

is rooted in, the gleaned
subsistence

filling my love
from floats and bockety carts
unloaded in
the haggard at Lughnasa.

2

The forefather I meet comes
crossing the bank through cow parsley
and meadowsweet.

The smear of the outhouse
on his clothes, he clears sops
from the hair of his poll.

Now that he's still nimble
from a life in outlying
fields and whinlands, my quest

would be to ask
after the last corncrakes,
the scythe that spared the nest.

But the bonds that make me proud
make me party to it all:
the quick incisions in a filthy stall,

gin-trap and snare, terror
of vermin, the hawk hanging from a pole
with broken legs, like twigs.

'I caught my fuckin' hand in it' —
a gruff relation, nursing
an ooze of blood from his thumb,

and passing: 'But I'll get the basthard yet.'
He rounds the shed
and disappears into his past,

leaving me to surmise:
the fox held in a fatal snag;
a deft blow putting him out.

3

The mute flowers of neglect grew
in the abandoned haggard, when I came
with a borrowed spade, and a dead cat
hanging from my hand.
I had no roots, no heavy creels to store,
no crackling swathes to prove a patient year —
an unseasonal wind rattled the elms
as I opened earth for a narrow grave.

A raven croaked above
the dead and the condemned,
telling the violations
and joyless reiterations, and I said,
'If, after famine, the land could know
the abundant haggards of care
let my seed know love again.
Let me be threshed and winnowed there.'

The Village Tailor

A man on the run from Lord Sheffield
took refuge in the carr
and built himself a reed-shanty.

He bent pins to barbless hooks,
then set lines of tailor's thread,
like tense spider-web, in plash and pool.

Coarse fish were his staple,
his world, muck up to the shin
where mud-bird and gallinule lived;

he slept little at night in the fen,
surrounded by nocturnal life:
chirp of moorhen, boom of bittern.

Poor Bob was a-cold in his marsh of refuge
as the well-fed bailiffs galloped by
on firmer ground.

To no avail
the cunning-woman came with cakes
and a plea to submit to the Lord —

he took only the food
and went wading back into the rushes,
towards toads and birds.

They found him crawling on all fours,
almost crab, mad from swampy nature.
Some overcame their fear to minister to the creature.

Going Back

We're driving off —
an angry car abandoning
the yard, as cottage doors
close after us. The old
wash our plates in vacant rooms,
scour the pans of soured affections,
and resume their vigils
by the soft clocks of memory.

We're driving away
from the rutted tracks
in a craft that keeps us
from land and rain.
Too late now to go back,
the small road
conducts our haste
to the tense carriageways we maintain.

We're driving on
past the first warehouses
of the city we espouse.
No random logs or bones,
no sudden hoards
disturb our neat trajectory
over the smooth concrete
to suburbs of lost history.

We drive down
into the eve of new lives
where the old home haunts us
like a holiday.
A child sleeps in the rear seat,
sure of the future we make.
Behind him charred bridges
to quiet fields, the chances we take.

The Clare Island Survey

1

I have the sketch of Clare Island,
in your hand. You drew the great brow
in silhouette from the mainland,
and scribbled gulls over a blue sound,
then etched a furze bush
with pencilled spikes in the foreground
and, in between, some trees, a slate roof
and a red gable huddling together.
No sooner had I left two years ago
than you made our trip, on your own, to Mayo.

2

It lures me back, seawards,
to a headland of thrift and stone
where July strikes cold with its bluster —
and already there's no getting away,
the native speakers are shouldering my boat
to the slipway. I float her
and fill her with my tackle (rain gear,
a sooty kettle), then pay the interpreter
and row out alone into heavy waters,
where the gulls come into their own.

3

So I turn to Clare Island, and approach,
as they line up on the pier
and jostle for place, the forefathers
ready to construe my coming,
unwilling to believe that I am strange
to the old score of grant and annexation.
And I step ashore, deaf to their questions,

my pages blank for the whims of day.
Here I will inscribe readings
for the Clare Island Survey.

4

Gillie or squire in the first photographs,
going far out to give the scale
with a yardstick as a staff,
remote, unnamed, a small notch,
I would be measured against you,
and will lose face, pacing out
in the footsteps of the early workers
to where fatigue compels the heart,
and return then, my face aglow
with a booty of old words, and new echoes.

Manx Shearwater

By day,
on the shore, during this year's holiday
we desired those distant, rocking waters
where shearwaters raft in thousands;

by night,
those islands where they come ashore
as weird calls teeming in the dark.
But, stronger than regret,

one evening,
love rose into us and robbed us of breath.
You knew then those shearwaters
that the storm spends, and wrecks far inland.

Kestrel

Took my eye into the air of himself
and threaded it,

sewing me to the sky
with his looped cycle of flight

up the gully,
then traced a noose

around a lowland belfry
and now, in the suburbs,

can needle a spot
above the apex of a gable,

draw the skein
in circles widening out,

and glide back
to the eye of his obsession.

Red Grouse

On a windy afternoon
fifteen years ago
we put on flapping jerkins
and set out across a moor

in North Tipperary,
my mother protesting,
my eye greedy
for the promised bird.

So I fly off alone
to a strange hollow over the hill
where the going gets rough
through *fraocháns* and heather,

where I nearly falter
with raindrops weeping
onto my waders —
when I hear it from the outcrop:

the grouse saying *go-back, go-back*;
and my father's
following calls
coming into range.

Curlew

The greyhound bolted after the hare
over ditch and bank
and up onto the hill
as if the hunt were to end in the air.

I strode across humble country
after her, with curlews
calling through a fine spray of rain
falling on upland fields.

I could stop to wonder how the light,
at the late hour, gathered
in the drops on the rush-flower
that were mild gems of grief,

if the gruff handler's heart
lifts, with the dog he has slipped,
towards the scruffy land.
As I followed into the gorse

I weighed the curlew with misgivings.
There was the bitch,
her nose in the grass,
sniffing the hare's absence.

Guillemot

You'll have seen me pointing to a bird
among gannets on a cliff
and heard me say *guillemot*,
in the guise of a maker.

I want you to have that name
for the first time,
to say it again
if our love stays unbroken.

If we part
it will have been a word
between two boats at sea
after their oarsmen have spoken.

Cuckoo

Scarcer now
than when he named himself
to every meadow in the townland
when the hay was down,

as I stood on the butt of the wain,
bedding in what tumbled from the pikes
with *cuck-oo*
repeated from the next acre.

So I drifted off
to stalk nearer the bird.
The song got louder
along the bristly edge of the headland.

I hadn't said a word
when my uncle came
calling 'Seán!'
and so I lost the cuckoo.

Skylark

A shard of mirror on the moor,
an image in the grass,

brought the skylarks
down from heaven

and changed their songs
to little squeaks on glass.

Meadow Pipit

Or *reafóg*, as my father said,
when the small bird on the sward
ran away with its splayed
wing twitching,

not in pain
but to divert us
from the brood
in the core of a tuft.

And we left,
this much the wiser:
that the little ones
needed us gone.

Now my plane flies in
from where they call them
Wiesenpieper,
and splays both wings to stop.

Away from the airport,
I stalk back
to low pleadings
at the edge of earshot.

Wren

While the valley is filled with rain
I recall the lip of the wren's nest,
how its fine wattle of brittle stalks
couched and housed my forefinger.

I imagine shelter from deserted fields,
sad clocks and dripping cables.
My streaming windows wait —
until the sun cleaves to glinting hedges

and a child in wellies splashes at the gateway
where the frost once shattered underfoot.
That was Stephen's Day
and the King of the Birds was dead.

Now his song explodes in a briar bush.

Chough

With the tower-builders gone from the promontories
I can inspect the fallen stairs,
the chimneys clogged with mortar and twigs,
no gyre there for my late ascendant.

So I go out again and cross
sheep pasture to the edge of the cliff
where the choughs are riding on the updraught.
Their voices are the squeaky hinge

of a door yanked open on old atrocities.
When they settle
they displace old tenants of the castle,
Macbeth's mad wife, and Yeats

looking down on small fields inland —
even Malachi Mulligan.
Their bright lobster bills
are a beacon only for themselves.

Twite

A scant party of finches
is blown across a winter shore
to settle, out of sight.
Follow them, then,

along the wrack of the storm-line.
Let the flowerlets gone to seed
and the trembling grass stalks
that they feed on

be the décor of our days.
These end in a gust across shingle
snatching those twites
back to a darkening coast,

and leave us our subsistence in this:
that as the waves unfold towards night
our mouths will taste
the licking-salts on our sea-brows.

Coda

Evening on a spit of rock and gravel,
kelp and wrack at the verge, my favourite bay.
After the taut mirror of tide, levels
slacken, then the surge goes racing from me.
The shingle drains, the birds are moving out
over a last concurrence of waters
to feed. Tonight I could be free of them.
My coat flaps and shudders on the wearer,
knocking to know if I am any more
than trail, convergence, go-between.
Creatures that were seen are now flying
out of range, so I must be fledged, in turn,
into convictions that no bird can help
as I take to the empty air, and dare myself.

Field-trip to Inishmore

1

We called our coming to the island
a field-trip for breeding birds,
with binoculars and recording cards,
the two of us savouring our own
space on the throbbing deck
as the cutting prow spawned
an aftermath of foam behind us.

2

The west had broken into a bright idea
as clear mountains rimmed
the tremendous, shimmering plain of the sea,
and alive in all of this
was an island with its own commotion
of diesel, rusted metalwork, mini-vans
and robust, undisciplined children.

3

And there were men waiting
to manage our play, with bikes
we jockeyed over, then mounted clear
of the craft shops at the harbour
to the small three-cock hayfields,
the stone walls, and the stony roads
jolting the island into us.

4

The place we stayed in opened
onto the sea and the sea's air,
no solid house, but a timber,
breezy hostel called Dún Aengus
because the god got tired of stone
and wanted this creaking, sleepless
dormitory as his summer home.

5

Sea-birds were the pretext that drew
us out one evening: manxies,
stormies, that come ashore at night
to the heaped boulders at the end
of land, when the lonely couple
in the last farm puts out the light
of dialect until the morning.

6

Less plausible observers,
wheeling our bikes down to the blustery
shore, we heard no petrels
over the cold sea we had come to;
only at the dark, concrete slip
a currach like a basket at our noses
offered the stench of absent fish.

7

Still, the limestone pavement
glowed to those exacting eyes
that closed on our instinctive kiss,
like an otter on the outer islet
that lives on out of sight.
He licks his paws undisturbed,
and goes unrecorded.

A Field Guide

This script is a willow
bending in the breeze
of a June evening.
But don't take my word for it.

Watch the pressure and slack
of the new shoots yielding,
then giving back to themselves.
Who knows what you might see

among the pollarding?
Volatile eyes winking from the trees,
and in an old wren's nest —
look, a mouse!

Surely a river flowing slowly,
mirroring light,
where the earlier mists
meant that the night had been other.

And maybe, someone coming downstream
with a split-cane rod,
a mere boy whose boots
are slapping the irises

as he strides out to meet you.
Now be warned. This young
innocent will reveal himself
in a slip of the tongue.

Scarecrow

1

The gruff farmer calls up the children,
the meek ones leaping through a meadow
of flowers whose names they don't know,

and at his bidding they disentangle from weeds
what lies fallen at the back of an outhouse,
or salvage things from the ash-heap:

jam-crocks, porter-bottles,
a step-ladder with missing rungs,
kettle-hooks, and cauldrons.

Then they leg-over a dormant gate
to cross into vistas of stiff corn
and crows that veer off instinctively.

This is where I begin in the planted field
as whatever they drive into the ground,
scaffold and clothe, assemble, and tie down.

Say the old step-ladder cloaked
in a woollen coat, my face a steering wheel
that speaks in tinkles of glass on glass.

2

They come again the following year,
the kids wading through vetch
and loosestrife. They are carrying

packaging from a building site.
A boy lobs a small, hard bottle ahead
into the unknown and runs on to it,

then follows the other boy and a girl,
truant through the gap, into the barley field.
The crow-scare detonates.

Whatever I was has reduced to place
and direction where hedge meets hedge
and a power cable sags above a gateway.

To take my stand in the waving grain
I entice along tight corridors of corn
to the usual zone of assembly

and come duly, a light snowman of polystyrene
with a polythene cape and a nose-bottle,
baptised with pee as they giggle.

3

The contractors leave engines running
as they open gates to the wheat field
and pitch scarecrows onto the headland.

I'm shifting gears towards the sea
on an old river of road
that winds past the strategies of land —

acreage, injustice, loss —
to where the farmers come
after harvest, to observe the offing.

Here's bric-à-brac for the sea-trove
as these white feet
toe their line along the shore.

Shells, stones,
beaks and skulls,
driftwood fluted or full of holes,

a little wave-worn slab of teak
with its brass lifting-ring —
a tiny door opening on an origin —

all these fill up my window sill.
I have made my own inventory
out of the immense volume of the sea

to have a list, to be sure,
a line of measured rungs,
a clef where things are sung.

Next in Line

1

The old man had struggled to fix him.
He lodged the timber well down into the earth,
so he rooted in the hoed ground;

then he filled out, as young men do,
and grew into his collapsed clothes —
and one morning he was gone,

probably caught an early trawler,
leaving only the print of recent shoes
that moved off from where he had stood.

And who could blame him? With carrots
being unsocketed from the loam, and cabbages
having their heads removed, and potato eggs

being levered out from underneath them —
with the lines shortening for the winter
table he might have been the next in line.

2

During his years away it was rumoured
in his place that he was cavorting
with this thin woman who you'd think

was made of rags and timber, and him laughing
and pointing to his inoculation mark:
'That was where he nailed me to a lath.'

That kind of thing has foreign echoes
on the mild island, especially when October
closes in, and stalks are ruined on the drills,

and the rooks strut proudly with dibbling
bills all over the cottage gardens.
The old man's style grew abstract,

he stuck plastic from the sea,
and sea-bird wings, and the tubes of spent flares
into the mesh of refuse filament.

If not enough to scare a bird
it was a store the beachcomber could hoard
against the bite of memory.

3

Then the excitement, one springtime, hurrying
over the sea! The new ferry flew
the kites of white gulls after its cargo

coming home, and one man standing
astern searched the water's surface
for some secret kept by the fishermen

as the terrified auks pattered away.
At the pier he jumped the gap to stardom —
and why not? It was a famous day

to widen even the narrow, marbled
eyes of the old islander
and invite him into the sunlight.

For too long he had been face-down
over the garden of fluffy
carrot-tops, potatoes, tapered onions,

that jetsam scarecrow; and these now hosted
his first creation, who chatted
too eagerly where he had sown.

But he knew it was now up to him
to say whose hands had weeded the earth
and planted the first seed in the greening rows.

The Fishing Hook

A hook I baited twenty years ago
in a Kerry summer was baited again
when it got overlooked in my uncle's *sugán* chair.
Since then it's held an unseen line
to me on the river bank, up to my waist
in irises and sedge. I would have waited
an age, from the collapse of the cast
into the gleam of the water, to the promise
of what pulled, under those evening reflections;
and waited on Christ, perhaps, striding down
that clear avenue of alders on dusty feet,
or the trembling needle that kept its head
on the meniscus during the science hour;
and waited still until the other evening
when she said 'What's this?' as she was sitting
with the hook's question between her fingers.
Then the memory took it, the line tightened,
and I was child's play on my own, thin lure.

Catching Blackbirds

My uncle made my first blackbird trap.
The crib was a latticed pyramid
as high as my knee. It was set

on a hooped rod and a *gabhlóg*
so that the lured bird would topple
the lid of the cage on itself.

'Are there any rules?' I wanted to know.
'No rules. Just get 'em.
That's the only shaggin' rule.'

So I baited the trap, and waited.
Next morning (I had almost forgotten)
a blackbird was bouncing in the fallen crib

and I was brave enough to reach
under the rim and grab my songster.
He was all prey, all blackbird

that I was ready to display to kin
except for one wisp of dry grass
caught above his left eye, marring him.

But when I reached a finger to remove it
he exploded in screeches,
his beak a stabbing compass;

my shocked hand recoiled. Then he was gone
back to his brood, to his vigils
in the berried ivy, to his pure song.

Now I'm drawn back to that snare
and my uncle's rough words, translated
as the grasp that feels the sinews

and the pulse of the heart, and holds.
So I walk in again, with small straws
on my clothes to tell where I've been.

The Flora of County Armagh

There are new flowers
in the hills of south Armagh,
new army towers
with revolving radar.

The deep-coloured stems
of the willow-herbs make them greater
than the plant in my garden.
These, and other slovenly species

sprawl about the base
of those igneous ridges.
Botany brings me north
for only the second time,

to name the flora
in the famous northern line:
how they fill the hedges of native
farms, and clog up ditches,

with the stamens of radar
on the new ones above
turning on themselves eternally.
Unloved, unloved, unloved.

Trove

You can walk from the door
across two sloping fields
to the barbed-wire fence of the ditch.
Climb over it,
and you're into the taller growth beyond.

Out there on the waterlogged land
you conjure up your own seismic centre.
Jump on the spot where you stand
to see how wide the ground shakes.
Call it a day to remember.

But if you know this to be the case,
why the fox's skull in your pocket,
and the lost wing-feather?

Declensions

1

A man straddles the 3-D, watery space
between a hard pier
and a shifting thwart
as he stows cases for transport;

and he stows the thole pins, the oars,
the solid gunwales, the laths,
the elver-trail of stitching on the sail's hem,
all in the tarred hull of the vessel sustaining them.

Like a currach being hauled
by craftsmen over a rough sea,
language sinks into a trough
and peaks again miraculously,

a tiny black boat diminishing
on the wide sea of story,
with words for weather,
for seaweeds, for stonechat, for flotsam.

2

While the men are away,
a woman walks to the end of her house
with dregs in a zinc basin.
She launches a ragged line of spray

into space. Before it vanishes
in the grass she imagines
the flexing cast of her husband's seed
in their early years.

Her diviner's arms relax. For an instant
she holds a wide ring in her lap,
like Sheela na Gig grasping
the lids of the eye of the storm,

where seas pile up
and seasoned men are overwhelmed
as they ride the waters
for a word they wanted from her.

3

A local surfer rides ashore
on the churning rim of a wave
and steps down into the foam
to hoist his gliding board

under his arm. There's that dizzy
space as the water slides back
between his toes and the whole island
takes some time to compose itself:

a deserted stretch of beach
with its marram hair-piece, a slatey sky
and a sharp bouquet of sea-holly.
Here's our suited rider with his stride

threshing through the dry sand
and his bright board with its fin,
as Arion survives the drowning sea
and carries home the dolphin.

The Marram-clocks

The hanging stalks of marram
rest their tips on the sand
like minute hands, and the wind
spins them round in a compass.

Scribes of a lost language,
they emerge during gaps in rain
to tell their own time
on the brighter, fictive days.

Before the next shower
speckles the dry slopes of the dune
you wonder what they might be in tune
with: are they the signatures

of some declining witness,
or the characters of the sea,
or the notation of scenery
with windy space translated?

But they also mean nothing.
When all the grassy hands
are busy on the dry sand
perfecting their own forms

they're still the measure of themselves.
If their energy is glee
it brightens in some analogy
still waiting for invention.

And it won't amount to home
when nothing that they trace
will outlive the whirling race
of sand blown from the shore.

Then the sky darkens on the site
with returning rain; this blocks
all those marram-clocks
from telling any more deeply.

A report has taken shape
before we understand
what's written by the wind
in the given hieroglyph

at an unmanned coastal station,
where the heroes of another story
ran towards the hissing sea
among sea-birds lifting, and leaving.

Map-maker

When the land was fenced off
as surely as bolting a gate,
this stranger arrived one day
on his bike and opened the same gate

again. Then he walked his first
spider-line over the fields.
They took him for a tourist
until he appeared

two days later on the brow
of the hill, to follow the back
of the wall he had fronted before.
When it rained on his map

a cover of clear plastic
kept him going, like a terrier
on the scent of a hare, and he turned
so close to his earlier spoor,

trampled stalks of grass
unbending in his absence,
that he followed his own departure.
So the finished map leaves spaces

in the fractal, for your own turn
some afternoon with the frosted ground
as white as paper and the sky
so free you could enter legend.

Erris

When the first seal spoke in that language she mastered
the whole barony swam in the lens of her eye.
They heard the seal's cries as the cries of their own kind,

so they tried naming heathers and the strange fish
they found turning speechlessly in the net's cradle.
But there was still that sky that wouldn't stay the same

and too many hills scarcely deserving their names
and, besides, what use to you will that ever be?
The seals deserted with the running shoal of tide

like weather that refused to pose for the painter,
and the tongue writhed out of the mouth in its struggle
with visa applications and subsidy forms.

The eel was finally free of folklore to cross
the shorn meadow on its way to the sea. The stoat
hid from the haymakers. The one-eyed deity

abandoned the mountains and came down their aerials
more reliably than when, in the high places,
the hilltop fires lit their stoops and flickering faces.

The Gulf Stream

for Derek Walcott

On an instinct not to be denied
the eel-fry leave your ocean, Master,
and swim homing into my childhood

where I lived near the teeming river.
I have gathered enough at low tide
to be called back to the open coast

you save from freezing by your cadence.
One of your logs, lying on Cross Strand
with its delicate frills of bivalves,

was delivered from your epic island.
Those little hangers-on were like sails
for a thinnest fleet that the shoreman

raises now for his own occasion
as he floats that log and trusts the waves
to lift him in the sea's true scansion.

Achill

Tradition has it that Achilles rested here
in a small cottage after his Trojan labours.
No one knows exactly where. The sea-breezes scour
the open land and eradicate the memory
of how he stood before his glamorous trireme
with his hero's crest.
                          Then, he put on pampooties
as he went to help the local men unloading.

His gold helmet was put above the mantelpiece
to gather ten years' dust.
                          It became the story
of how a local man called Harry O'Deasy
came back from England unannounced. He found
his farm run down, his dog neglected, his best
cattle sold — and so on. Of course you know the rest.

Corncrake

This spring the corncrake
signalled its lonely morse
for a love-pledge broken.
Its voice became remorse,

the corncrake taking the blame
for its virtual disappearance.
'I wasn't strong enough,' it said.
'I wasn't committed to endurance.'

Last night we listened at the fields
and missed the pleading sound.
The bird of passage had moved
from the faithless ground

and left a silent iris.
Somewhere else its grief
to another flower tonight
will call its petals soft, its season brief.

from *Limerick*

I A SIGN OF PEACE

A peregrine sallies from the cathedral spire
and glides to the corner of the sky's page. Then
it works strong wings rapidly along a line.

I feel the skein of history between us,
where a browsing deer hears the first strokes of the axe
in Cratloe, then runs off from Dunraven's beagles,

to be captured by her ladyship's aquarelle.
Gate-lodge and gate are still there in many places
to mark the passage of hunters and painters

when a falcon's flight commanded empty spaces.
Now the needle of a plane pulls its double thread
across the azure afternoon and lets it fray

for those who stay here beside the wide estuary,
with otters and wildfowl pictured in the parlour
as a sign of peace. Three mallard fly up the stairs,

snipe and woodcock are copied onto crockery,
an amateur sun is framed in my cousin's hall
and she says, 'Come in,' in the accent I know well.

2 IN WEST LIMERICK

My Latin primer was like a prayer book at
Grandad's wake. I read *amo, amas, amat*
to myself dutifully. The country people sat

around me drinking porter or tea, while outside
the pile of towels burned poorly because of the rain.
Noreen's eldest was in the middle of exams

and Joe's last prayer that night would help the boy succeed.
'If you have any faith at all . . . ' I was left to
learn the verb *to love*. Before they closed the coffin

I was told to put down my book and look at him
in the room. He was the wit of Islanddanny,
Joe Walsh. He had heard the shots of Gort a' Ghleanna,

he had known a woman who'd been through the famine.
Then the men carried the coffin down to the road
on a wretched evening with soot-black clouds.

I remember how the coffin handles glowed
through the twilight, like the golden bough Aeneas
carried to the underworld. That was a few years

later, Book VI of *The Aeneid*, the hero's
quest with the Sibyl from Cumae, the winning steps
through a grammar that's remote and elemental,

like my first memories of an old man in his seat:
me biting into an apple he had given me
and then him asking, 'Well, boy *bán*, is it sweet?'

4 A STONE'S THROW

Released to the summer sea, we played skimming stones.
Each small discus hit eight, nine, or maybe ten times
before it faltered. We threw in the direction

that the planes were headed, taking off from Shannon
with their privileged set returning to the States.
We knew our station then, and used fragments of slate

or other well-shaped bits of stone for our scansion.
If you angled well on a calm stretch of water
you could extend the count to the syllables in

the British Overseas Airways Corporation,
that alexandrine along the length of the plane
we waved to the day Paddy went back to Boston.

He threaded the first path my stones were longing for
to America, to see myself checking in
with words to make the stone take off as metaphor.

Gale Warning

after Günter Grass

The storm blew from the west after a gale warning.
No dead this time, but many fallen trees,
damage to property, and fears of global warming
compounding our general unease.
This wide world has us jaded. Will we be able
to stay the course at the rich men's table,
or will our stocks come tumbling down
if this uninvited weather stays in town

to make itself at home? — like the foreign flood
that have the gall to want to mix their blood
with the fair, unblemished bodies of this state
so that we have another, not ourselves, to hate.
More storms are forecast for the coming nights.
They know no bounds, they knock, and demand their rights.

Horses at Corratowick

The horses were a surprise to the man,
a group of five with a foal on the flank of a hill,

standing dense at the gate
in the brown dough of ground

they had kneaded under a tree.
Whereas the man understood other steeds and horsemen,

these ones stayed
in the naked harness of mid-winter.

They rested at the source of steaming air
and had no mind for smashing branches then

or the next morning
when he came back with the camera's eye.

They were too small to take
unless he got in with them

by climbing the bars of the gate
and getting their view of the back of a farmhouse.

So he staggered
on the broken slope as it fell into the valley,

taking him close to themselves,
but they didn't enthuse for the god of the sugar-cube —

they were grazing another peace,
their mouths welded to land,

their own vital organs
packed inside like Greek soldiers.

The buff stallion
dressed up the leaves of his ears at the whirr of the shutter,

a mere wren of a click,
not a man shouting with a black plastic stick,

or a man checking a fetlock.
The stallion drifted away to join the others

as the man watched them
with his naked eye,

until the mindless horses won
and the man twitched on.

Summer

So we were all eyes at the window-eyes
as we scanned the hedges for their story.
It was mid-winter, and we improvised
with beds on the floor and borrowed deckchairs.
Then we found the rudiments of the year,
the golden saxifrage and strawberry
flowering precisely in Lugnafahy.

The nearest spring gave a rhyme of water,
the element changing clear containers
into twin loads of brightness unconstrained
from well to table.

                    When a dog took off
cross-country, over the next field, a man
followed along the road calling 'Homer!
Homer!' The place answered to the summer.

Bertra

At the end of the day waves are tired.
The beach has been rinsed of its opinions,
and that dog now racing over the shore
will deprive it of even its shorebirds.
The place is guarded by planning controls
that the bay and the mountains adhere to,
and once you skirt the fence around the dunes
you're alone, keeping pace with your shadow.

That shadow, ready to float forever,
is held back by your footsteps as you search
for parallels among the tones of clay,
marram grass and shingle. Like you, it stops
at the cork dried out like last year's apple,
the yellow bulb forgetful of its use,
the brush worn to abstraction from the surf —
but fragments like these are never enough.

None of this jetsam could ever cohere
like the double pendulum of your stride
where regret is even with indifference
and the arrogance of blind conviction
alternates with a smile that sues for peace.
Either way, you still enact a passing
that's not the dog claiming an empty shore
or the seabirds either, which have to fly.

This evening you've come alone, so there'll be
no photographs of you in the landscape
beside an emotional sea. Nothing
will distract from the ordinary fact
of a man out walking during peacetime
in a style you've often admired, so slight
as he diminishes in the distance
and is almost lost in thickening light.

Merlin at Tarsaghaunmore

This is where the wizard lives,
still being realized
to cleave a range over the heatherings of a morning,
a surprise out of the mist.
This is where the horizon keeps an old nimble jack
away from the chattering city,
so no one can repute him to a bad end,
and no industry can exile him any farther.

He needs nothing more than the posts
he nominates with his feet,
this wire, this river bank,
this facing of stones to accommodate his desert eye,
and these two foxholes on the far side,
the stops of a flute he plays
when he lifts the glittering river.

But could you find him if you looked?
There has to be another god to upstage,
a different day that starts with maps,
and just as you stop for a eucharist of sandwiches
suddenly Pipit, the redeemer, is gone —
and there he is, with the mountain on his shoulders!
He's carrying the valley's only song!

A Midge Charm

Breeze god
    get up and scatter the armies of the itchy witch

Rain god
    ruin their gathering veil

Cloud god
    forbid this travesty of your image

Horse god
    shake your heathery mane

Water god
    splash your frown of ripples

Hill god
    lead us out of all hollows

Turf god
    preserve us with your smoke

Frost god
    put on your white coat
    and lock them all away!

A Discovery

August, an evening, and I'd had enough
of the meandering river's question.
That web of fields and abandoned walls
in the valley's upper reaches were in my fatigue
with the stone's character of toil and heartbreak
as the lidded evening thickened and I took
the peat of the river bank in my booted stride.
I walked *andante*, to the metronome of an ending,
when another crossed the twilit footbridge
con brio, in his day's closing passage,
making for a grassy patch near the river
and unloading a bulky pack of gear.
Who was this loner setting up for the night?
He had, of course, reached his wilderness
just as I was passing under cover
of the river's noise on the rising turf-bank opposite.
I supposed he wasn't there to be hailed
or challenged by someone who had got there
earlier, who would spoil an original story,
and I kept going, so as not to be seen.
And yet, here are the prints in that peat,
that steady exhalation where a range is stored
of a river diminishing to the cold
of spawning water at the top of its catchment.
The camper could have looked up from his preparations
to read the figure disappearing downstream
who had, in his turn, established his own pitch
where he imagined no one had been watching.
I held my pace steady in my aloneness
and never looked back until now, to revise
that favourite valley into a stage for eyes
and to realize how happily I walked
into the script of my own occasion.

The Drover's Stick

in memory of Paddy McHugh

Following on from your stories —
how you drove your cattle

through the night-roads to the fair —
you brought out your stick collection

and gifted me what I asked for,
the one I have to keep,

a hazel newly cut from the roadside
in Nephin's shadow.

Its white eyes peep
where someone planed the stems.

If I never make your miles
along your moorland river

this drover's stick
will remember another pace

as it seasons in the corner
within the busy house.

I take its weight again
and test its swing in the air,

like the wand you waved at dawn
when you conjured your given way

and drove those thirsting shoulders on
towards the lightening horizons.

from *The O——*

2

Among the O——'s beginnings there's this stream
that leaks from a gully on a remote mountainside.
A hag overlooks the place, with its top of heather
silver-stemmed with age, and a peaty bank
like an old cow releasing the first water.
There's a single oak there too,
surviving in the shelter of a cutting carved by the stream,
and an old crow's nest built from fallen
fingers of the tree. The trail sags like a hammock
into this crossing, where water pours over
stones, and you lose all birdsong under
the noise of running water. Only the raven
honks to say thanks for the leftovers.

A reminder, then, where a man bends down
to kiss the stream, that he meets an image
of his own thirst, framed in the shadowing sky.

3

The O——— was every river he'd lived by:
Owenmore, Owenglas, Owenwee,
Owenduff, Oweninny, Owengarve,
formed when a great bird stood in that valley
and left the emphatic print of its claws.
The spate had a channel from the high heather
to the estuary and its runway of water
where running salmon were crowded.

Between those two the river fought
the outline of its fated course.
                                        It meandered
over its basin and made silted pastures
in the loops where hunger and folklore could survive.
The till of glaciers was sifted along its banks,
pine roots collapsed, the turf, in section,
dried and, still not content, the O———
abandoned one channel, to force its way
along another bed of land where fish could run.

After a dry spring, when honeysuckle
raised its shoots in despair, you'd wonder
where the next flood would come from.

It was hard to think that these stale pools
could host the urgent passage of warriors from the sea.

4

It was the same sea reshuffling the shore
at the windward edge of the sandy cemetery,
and the same ground where his bones used to rest
until one January storm finally made a break in the wall,
and the Council knew that history had a formidable enemy.
On winter tides a seal would appear
out of the surf to check the progress of skulls
and other bones falling from the bank, until the head
itself was threatened that had sung it all one time.
And then it happened, that dull, unavoidable
commotion of the damned ocean pounding at the base
of those small grains of comfort he had come to love,
saying, 'This is the time now to release yourself
back to those waves where all life began.'
And the skull fell into the foam, and floated
where the flounder and bass ran in the shallows.
When another wave came, and it smashed,
it could have settled into the small mercy of sand.
But a fish had been alerted. And that was enough.

6

The river ran the last stages of its journey
over stones that waves had heaped up
across its mouth, the wild sea being stronger.
This evening, as surfers packed up to go home,
a high tide was pushing foamy waves
closer to the lip of the bar, and in the commotion
of surf and brown waters of the river's spate
sea trout were ready for migration.
They had braved it to the very top of the waves
where manes of water were being scattered
by a westerly breeze.
      They knew from the taste of the bay
that this was the time to move.
        When the next high wave
brought water over the bank of shingle
a few fish managed to riffle through.
Others, hesitating, saw tail-fins
disappear into the gloom of the surge
and they realized what instinct meant.
With their white flanks flashing at the surface
more and more of them rushed through into the O———
on each successive pulse of the racing sea,
until the tide turned and a moon was left
above the shimmer, wondering what had happened.

16

The river was rain,
                    then rain for a second day.
All weather lore went limp, like a damp page.
The sky was level with his frown.
                                    The air bounced.
The dripping heather and every shining stone
for fourteen miles were flowing towards the sea
through the passage of a famous spate stream.
All over the catchment the day said flood.
Tons of water hammered past the house.
A brown monster writhed across the fields,
raging to be over, to settle back to the sea,
to be again the scullery maid of the bog,
the whole summer washing the glacier's stones.

The foam came down in fluffy stacks,
white and stiff like catering hats.
Sand martins flew past their sunken homes,
but the sheep under the whin weren't interested
in flowers wasted, buttercups gone under.
Long brambles snagged with baler twine
trailed dead grass across her countenance!

And then, abroad in the grey dawn, alone
on the moor, an angler moved through all of this,
carrying a silver salmon hanging from his fist
in fulfilment of its own weight of light.

21

There must have been a fault in the rock where the spate
had scoured out such a heavy reservoir.
Anything waiting within would sleep on a dream
of drift and pine-roots at the base of earth.
Day came into focus as a silted crag.
Now and then the head of a tinker's horse
ghosted on the surface.
                              Then the labour of rain.

He stripped line from his protesting reel
and tested the air above the pool.
                              He cast.
The fly tracked the dark water
like a satellite on its course among the frozen stars.
Lifted out at the end, it was flailed again,
taking a second purpose close to the first.
He watched it with his faith
that something had run so far upstream
when the flood was on.
                              Suddenly, the fly locked.
A boil had spread where it had swum alone.
He lifted the rod and a salmon was on,
moving deep within the mountain's shadow.
He had no net, and no one to call to.

22

For a long time the salmon refused to show. She ran
tense under the taut line where a fine V
revealed the position of the nylon.
He would steer her around the pool, keep her
clear of the snags on the far bank, but not haul —
he'd lost a good springer that way once.
He gave her time, and line when she needed it.

Then the reel screamed, and she breached, appealing
to the air that had given her the spate.

Her silver flank sank again.

She went patrolling the pool for the key to a puzzle
she had never known before —
                                such a small
buzz in her house, threatening everything!
To have made it all this way, to have survived
so many comrades taken in the mesh
of drift-nets, and then — betrayed at home!
What was it she hadn't sensed in that shrimp,
that little orbiting impostor?
They had taken zillions off Greenland
all winter. So why not snap at this,
for old times' sake? But to meet the ghost
of the mesh again, or a seal's hungry soul!

No, no, no, said her shaking head.
She clattered and thrashed,
                                clattered and thrashed,
as the heartless sheep continued to graze
and a raven flew over in its own life.

24

There she was, a three-pound grilse,
neutered now in his gravity, shouldered
into the grass. Caught. He grabbed
the neck, and levered out the fly.
The salmon made a choking noise
as if to say something that water understood
but could not be uttered in the element of air.
If fish squealed like rabbits he couldn't
kill them, but he was looking round for his priest,
or a stone, to knock her on the head and turn this life
into a dinner, as he had so many smaller trout,
when he hesitated.
                              Return that life. Show
the restraint you preach. Don't take her now and cancel
the passion you have known. Continue the story,
like those fine hen fish you put back
last year, restoring them to their life's chapters.
They were not any less yours for being saved.

Oh! It was time! It was time! She was losing breath!
Her pulse was fading!
                              The leaves of her gills were nearly
gone when he hoisted her body and rushed her
to the stream, standing astride her, until she shook
gently out of his hands to refuse him,
and then fade into the depth she came from.

from BIRD SWEENEY

Leavings

His name
a sibilance of aspens,
his mark there in mud,

hoof-prints of a stag
that galloped into absence
in this wood

and left a downy plume
adrift in mid-air,
leavings we follow

as we hunt ahead of death to hear,
beyond our bated breath,
his breath.

The Wood at Dusk

The row with Ronan should have steeled him,
but it made him shy instead.

He avoided the obvious trees
when they went searching for him.

When they raised their poles with banners
Sweeney skulked in a grove of bracken,
a woodcock they would never find.

So they called it a day and left.
An hour later, at dusk,
he was roding over the canopy.

North Tawton

Sweeney flew on
to a yew tree
in North Tawton.

The church steeple was the shape of a witch's hat.
Everyone in the village
was dressed in black.

A hearse prowled across the square
with a seaman's coffin
draped in a Union Jack.

Then Sweeney surged into the blue
above them, a dove in mourning.

He jingled the keys of a robin's song
beside a gardener.

As a house sparrow
he arrowed into their eaves.

He mimicked the stars among their starlings.

When he flew back withershins
among the swallows they took no notice.

The blackbird answered his blackbird calls.

Even a tawny owl was taken in
by a note he commandeered from a woodpigeon.

But when he came to the crow
he couldn't find any black.
They had taken it all for the mariner's funeral.

The best he could manage was a grey mantle.

At once the crows saw through his disguise
and mobbed him over the hill.

The Hawk in the Orchard

A sparrowhawk flashed through the orchard
on the line of a previous sparrowhawk.
His centred eyes and instrument of feet
holding the thrush almost too far down
for the hooked bill to reach
told Sweeney how his kill would be.

The thrush was in the hawk's fate
as it flailed the evidence of shells
on a makeshift anvil. Lynchseachan
could piece together how it had happened
where his slow, obscure footsteps
led to feathers in the silvered grass.

It may have been him who first spoke
the hawk in the orchard, having seen it;
and then Sweeney, on the trail of his follower,
finally shot past everything into his own
appearance as the panic of the orchard,
such was his hunger to come level
with what he had foreknown.

Sweeney in Erris

Sweeney sang in a grove of pines
as light skidded off a rippled pool.

A river lost its sweetness seawards.
Oak-leaves gathered on rainy cobbles

where an empire had passed.
Already too late, he sang through the surf

of a windy wood.
Antiquity had been here once. She wrote:

sea trout running every summer,
loaded with stars.

But light and water took them
to be the ghosts of their glen

in the otherworld of a river,
the raven lording.

Now only a linnet was allowed
in a company of thistles.

One rowan couldn't redeem
and was too much to condemn,

rhododendron too deeply rooted
in its own bitter shadow

for anyone to bother. Thistledown
flaked from Sweeney's bill

and swept away to a vastness.

Sweeney Translates

I'm the first flight
under dawn light,
hen of heather,
mason of the egg.

Yellow on red,
siobhán of the fuchsia,
my song carries
in the blowy lane.

When they tried to fix
my wings to a crucifix
they couldn't decide
which quill was my wrist.

So I slipped the bite
of their cold pins
and sing again
within the song of myself.

The Burning City

Wader Sweeney
wanted to get to the burning city
but the river was wide at that point   he lost time

crossing over   taking both shores   downwind
he could smell the burning   he flew again
with a flock of undecided dunlins

they switched directions over dark water   he said
'No it's this way'   his words a redshank
scolding the others   he could smell the burning city

the main emotions   on the stiffening wind
pushing the wildfowl back he laboured on
upstream   'What about the kids
in the pleading city?'   his words a curlew

bubbling under the ideal note
when a farmer dropped a crowbar on a stone
the birds detonated in every direction

Sweeney wanted to shout 'It's upstream
to the smouldering city!'   'This way'
said the ringed plover's plaintive note

in all the confusion as the smell changed
and the first soldier kicked over the rubble
of the ruined city

One for Sorrow

At the prime time of May blossom
something grey shoots past at dusk,
hunched under the gloom,
impaired by memory.

Fated to survive,
it lords the lanes and callows,
folded in its robes on a post,
nowhere earning victimhood.

With the big house burnt
and the gamekeeper gone,
no one is left to nail it to its throne
and let it haunt like a god.

Sorrow, to be sure, in the elaborate
care of its preenings.
Without these it would not go far
through the galaxies of flies.

Once, badly shaken by a catapult,
it hove its kite out of parkland
and spent a night
as the eye of river alders.

Ever since, winged on its fear,
it glides down a margin of terror
to the end of a life,
no leisure to ask how one can

live like this, no conscience
to decode its screeching chatter,
whatever it is breaching the peace
of the ruined demesnes.

A Wagtail Gloss

Sweeney danced
      on the peak of a roof,

little alpinist in his crampons
      after a fly,

so high and light!
      Then he settled again,

ahead of his own long wobbling tail —
      only to vanish in a flit,

not caring how the scribe's pen
      had to labour after him

in his economy and freedom.